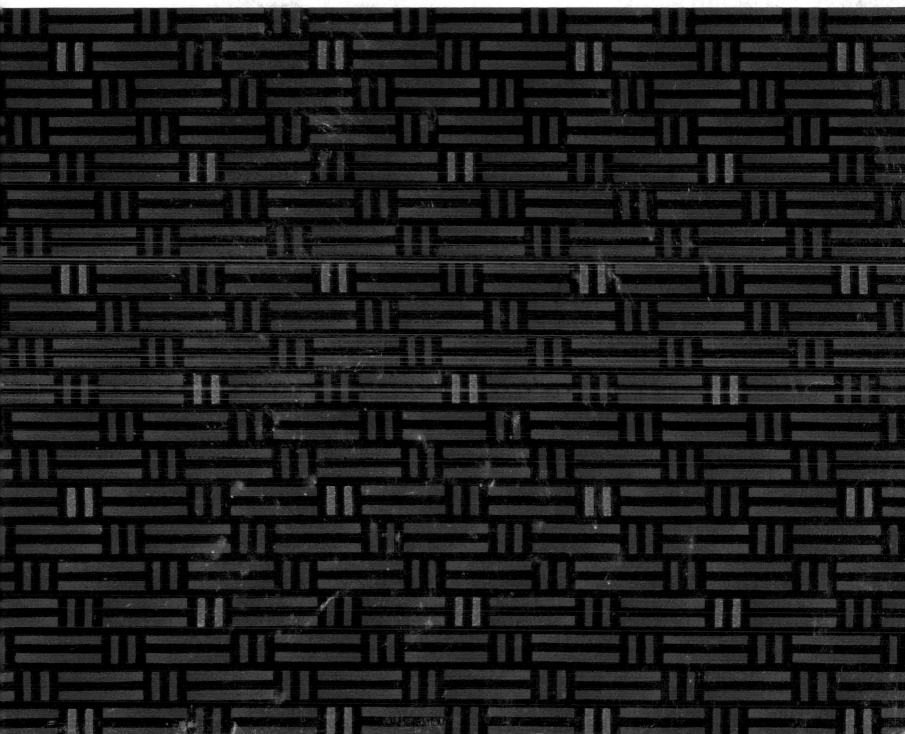

EPOUSTOUFLANT

EPOUST

OUFLANT

David Snyder

Photographs by
JON MILLER

Design by
DEBORAH DALY

FORMAN PUBLISHING, INC.
Santa Monica, California

In loving memory of my father, Hamar Snyder, for the creative spirit he instilled in my life.
To my mother, Mae King Snyder, for her continued support, confidence, and love.
And to Robert, a friend who has always been there.

Library of Congress
Cataloging-in-Publication Data:

Snyder, David, 1936–
Epoustouflant; the style of David Snyder/
David Snyder; photographs by Jon Miller.
       p.   cm.
     ISBN 0-936614-11-0; $39.95
     1. Snyder, David, 1936–
     2. Interior decoration—United States—
History—20th century.   I. Title.
     NK2004.3.S66A4   1990   90-3956
747.213—dc2D   CIP

10 9 8 7 6 5 4 3 2 1

Contents

Foreword, by Philip B. Miller   7
Preface, by Len Forman   10
Introduction, by David Snyder   11

Part One: A la Campagne

Charleston-by-the-Sea   17
Charleston Variation   24
Wicker by Lauren   25
Log Cabin Eleganza   26
Country Pied-à-Terre   28
Plywood House   30
Italian Log Barn   32
The Turquoise Room   36
Italian Villa   37
English Gothic   38
Bavarian House   40
Marella Agnelli Collection   46
Alpine Ski Lodge   48
High Country West   50
Santa Fe Lounging Bathroom   56
Mexican Festival   58
Chili Con Carne   59
Irish Ways   61
Souleiado Collection   62
Giverny House   67
French Country Barn   68
American Barn   74
Club Florida   78
Palm Beach Collection   84
Shibui Collection   92
General MacArthur's Quarters   100
The Crown and the Eagle   102
Casa de Campo   110

Part Two: En Ville

Sang-de-Boeuf   119
Christian Lacroix Quarters   124
Northern Italian Collection   126
Mark Hampton Collection   132
Eighteenth-Century Tradition   136
Avant Premiere   138
Blacks and Whites   144
Media House   146
Lycra Loft   150
Normandie Collection   152
Lesage   155
Vivere Italiano   156
Inexpensive City Opulence   162
The Green House   164
Starting Points   168
French Fantasy Dining   172

Part Three: Dossier

Shibui Shop   175
Christmas, European-Style   176
Focus: Scandinavia   177
Carnivale   178
Field's Afar   179
Formal Black and Cafe Noir   180
French Quarters and French Barn   181
The World's Finest   182
Marella Agnelli   184

Domestic Resources   187
Foreign Resources   189
Acknowledgments   192

Foreword

tyle. The word seems simple enough to comprehend, yet it is so often misunderstood. The mystery of it lies in the fact that though one immediately knows when style is present, its exact nature is difficult to analyze. Though classic in character, its distinction lies in its ability to surprise, reinterpret, reinvent.

One person who may be defined by such a word is David Snyder.

As I reflect upon our long friendship, I remember my first impression of David as a person who innately possessed the sort of style for which Marshall Field's is known the world over. And the longer I work with him, the more I grow to understand and admire his inimitable sense of the extraordinary, as I witness the creations born of his talent and their effects on the entire world of design.

David is truly a beacon of quality and style, a reservoir of unparalleled imagination. From the moment of his arrival at Marshall Field's, in 1979, David has been able not only to understand the vision indigenous to this great store, but to elaborate and enlarge upon it. He has done this through a vehicle of expression unique to Field's—the Trend House.

The concept of the Trend House at Marshall Field's emerged long before David came to us. (Actually, the first Trend House happened in 1936, the year David was born.) It was created as a means of showcasing affordable home design. You see before you a photograph of the Trend House in 1938, two years after its inception. That was only the beginning. Today, twice a year, in our State Street store, an entire suite of rooms is designed and built, complete with furniture, art, and fixtures, each one unique in concept and extravagant in execution. No longer merely a showcase of the possible, the Trend House has become a showcase of the imagination—a metamorphosis that has taken place at the gifted hands of David Snyder.

One of the early Trend Houses, 1938.

Trend House, 1958.

David Snyder, Sir Antony Acland, Richard Donat, and Philip Miller with His Royal Highness, the Prince of Wales, shopping in Field's Afar.

Though the vision has always been David's and David's alone, through the years he has found inspiration from a number of places and many willing collaborators, including some of the most highly respected talents in the home design field: Angelo Donghia, Mark Hampton, John Mascheroni, Marella Agnelli and Andrée Putman. He has also worked with Christian Lacroix and the Demery family of Souleiado to create rooms of extraordinary and peerless design.

One of David's greatest challenges has been to uphold the old traditions of quality and style, while introducing a profusion of new ideas and designs, revealing completely original thought. This he has done, and done so well, that he has in fact become one of the barometers of the design industry, not to mention a catalyst of home fashion—not only a finger on the pulse of that industry but actually providing the surge of the pulse itself. His designs are presented much like a runway fashion show in Paris, where one views a season's haute couture not as reality but as an inspiring ideal, a position taken to make a statement. From his Chile con Carne room—a clever juxtaposition of Victorian and Spanish—to his dining room as bistro, created expressly for the art of entertaining, David's work never fails to evoke a response or create a sense of wonder in all who witness it.

Thus, what you are about to view is more than a mere retrospective of David's work, it is a glance into the window of one man's particular vision. It should not surprise you, then, that you will not find a single room done purely in the Southwestern or English Cottage styles, but rather an eclectic mix that pleases the heart as much as the eye—and that reflects, throughout, David's trademark sense of humor and personal charm.

The unexpected is what one may expect from David Snyder. This quality, in part, is what makes him an artist of such high caliber, one who constantly challenges preconceptions and broadens our ideas of beauty. He has truly been a continual source of inspiration to me. I am sure you will find this glimpse into his work an inspiration as well.

Philip B. Miller
Chairman, Marshall Field & Company

Preface

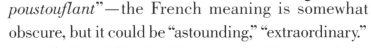

poustouflant"—the French meaning is somewhat obscure, but it could be "astounding," "extraordinary."

To David Snyder, "*époustouflant*" means "anything that knocks you out."

"I've always been bold," says David, "and I've broken the rules—in the sense of what I've thought the rules were. Life is all about experimentation and exploration. You have to let experience into your life and into your soul. Then you grow."

This philosophy translates into a unique design style that is relevant to all who are interested in making their environments right for them. "You can do your own thing," David stresses. "Just break the bonds that prevent you from taking that next step. Dare to be different."

David teaches by example. By studying his work, you can learn how to mix styles and colors, to see beauty in a perfect flower or in a simple line. He knows the value of texture—wood against stucco, terra cotta with silk. He understands the impact of elegance—of fabulous fabrics, and hand-carved screens, and gold leaf. And the importance of grand scale—one huge vase positioned against a painted wall might be more effective, and pleasing to the eye, than an entire collection of *objets*.

And David is eclectic—he believes in the importance of myriad styles. Use what you love, and even what you already have. Says David: "Start with one beautiful piece, and take it from there. You don't need clutter. And you can do anything you want to do. The potential is always out there for people to be what they want to be."

David's message is one for the nineties and beyond: *Learn to know your own mind, let your imagination soar, and dare to be different.*

Len Forman
Publisher

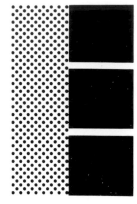

Media House.

Introduction

The publishers of *Epoustouflant* have asked me to try to describe my style. What is it? Where does it come from? Where do we go from here? And what does all this mean to you, the reader of my book, in your day-to-day life?

In each of us, a little of our childhood remains. It is, after all, in our formative years that we find the foundation for our personalities, our characters, our goals, and our tastes. This is certainly true of me.

My early years were spent in the farm country of Ohio. I can't remember a time when I wasn't fascinated by the way things looked—or a time when I didn't have strong opinions about how they *should* look.

My father, who, I realize now, possessed a strong aesthetic sense, had an enormous influence on the growth of my personal style. He was handy and creative, and I admired that very much. His hobby was to buy an old house and fix it up. The whole family would work together restoring a house; we scraped woodwork and did whatever had to be done. And sometimes my dad would let me decorate some of the rooms myself. I loved it, and knew even then just the effect that I was after.

But youngsters of my generation were expected to be something predictable and safe—a doctor, a lawyer, a businessman. I followed an acceptable route: college, with a science concentration, then the Air Force; but I still couldn't quite find my way. After the service, back at school at the University of Tampa and now majoring in fine arts, I realized that I needed to do what I wanted to do—not what I was supposed to do.

The creative world held enormous attraction for me. My first sculpture course was miraculous, and I would stay in the laboratory until ten at night. This wasn't work, but joy. I loved creating in three dimensions, and I liked building things.

With Marella Agnelli.

My dear friend, Lady Wedgwood of Barlaston, dares to be different!

11

George Philip Kelly, former CEO of Field's, Robert Estum, and Andrée Putman with the author.

Michael Yount and Randy Trull flank the author, conferring with Sybil Connelly, the Irish designer.

Gradually, it dawned on me that I really could experiment with my life. I was accepted at the Parsons School of Design in New York City. I was on my way.

What one might consider my growing-up years were spent at a succession of great department stores: Rikes in Dayton, Ohio; Abraham and Straus in New York City; the May Company and Robinson's in Los Angeles; and, finally, Marshall Field's in Chicago. During all those years, I never stopped learning: I learned the business; learned about American and European tastes and how they could be combined; and, most important, learned to make my fantasies come to life.

I've had a wonderful life up to now—it's been like a fabulous vacation. Because of the work that I do, I've had the opportunity to travel from one end of the earth to the other—France, Italy, England, Germany, Scandinavia, the Far East—and I'm not done yet by any means. I'm looking forward to an African safari and a visit to Russia.

Whenever I travel, whether in this country or abroad, I look and I absorb. It's fascinating to see what kinds of environments different sorts of people create. I've had the opportunity to be a guest in some of the great homes of Europe: It's a fabulous education for me to see how treasures are displayed that have been in some of the old families for hundreds of years. Though that doesn't happen very often in the United States—we are, after all, a young country—it has taught me the value of combining different styles and periods. It's okay to be eclectic in this manner, just as long as you love the pieces and they mean something to you.

So what is the style of David Snyder? Because my work is visual, it's a little hard to explain verbally. But certainly we can use words like "personal," "overscale," "eclectic," and "experimental."

I have spent my entire career examining the rules as they're understood by so-called experts—and then breaking them. There are so many choices that we can make in life—in the way we live and the way we create our environments—that it seems a pity to be tied into knots by what those self-styled experts might think. Along with all this, I do try to make my environments comfortable and livable—to make them accessible both to homeowners and to their guests.

The cornerstone of my design philosophy, I think, may be summed up by the phrase "theater of the home." As Shakespeare said, "All the world's a stage." I certainly agree with that. What better place could a person choose to be onstage than in his or her own home? Your environment is your creation, your stage set, and your life can be a work of art. You have the ability to design, to your taste, your own backdrop—a stage upon which you can most fully enjoy playing out the scenes of your life.

When I design a space, I usually end up with an eclectic mix of styles and colors. To be sure, it's important that there be some harmony among the various tones but you have to go with your instincts when considering the overall look. Think of a painter painting on canvas. The result might well be any assortment of shapes and colors. But the important thing is that it be exciting, interesting, and pleasing to the artist. Let those same criteria guide you in creating your own setting.

Oprah Winfrey shopping with David.

I am not a purist. Of course, I insist that the elements I choose be of good quality and right for my concept. But other than that, I might mix an eighteenth-century sidechair with a stucco-and-log wall, or some inexpensive Mexican baskets with one fabulous antique armoire.

Grand scale is one of my trademarks. I have always felt comfortable with those great knock-'em-dead pieces that can make a room. Simplicity goes well with overscale. You don't need a lot of pieces to create a dream room. I often go for the dramatic, for the one-of-a-kind. I also believe that less is definitely more: You might have several wonderful chairs, and a fabulous ceramic vase, dark-stained floors and dark-painted walls, with minimal additional furniture. Be imaginative in your choice of dramatic lighting and you've got a wonderful environment.

Good design in the style of David Snyder does not have to be expensive. But I do think that you should live as beautifully as you look—and

Anne and Philip Miller admiring one of David's Trend Houses.

that takes some hard work. You have to decide yourself what sort of backdrop you want to create, and you have to decide what you want your personal style to be. Don't be influenced by what everyone else is doing. Don't be afraid to try something new.

You do have to set up a budget. It might be many thousands of dollars, or it might be just enough for one well-made table. Buy what you like, but make sure it's of good quality. You want something that will last. You'll tire quickly of a trendy, trashy purchase. And remember that you don't have to do everything at once. Acquire things that you love as you can afford them.

And use what you already own. Do you have an antique quilt that has been handed down through the generations? Hang it on the wall and make it the focus for your room.

You ought to explore. You have to be open to experimentation. Most important, don't be afraid. If you allow diversity into your life, you will become a more interesting person. You will grow and become more confident. You can change your life, and in the process create a nurturing environment for you and your family — a home that is yours alone.

David Snyder
Vice President, Home Fashion Director
Marshall Field & Company

14

A la Campagne

The countryside is an ideal place to pursue the spirit of *époustouflant*. After all, everything in the great outdoors is larger than life—the skies are bigger, the trees grow taller, the air fills your lungs, the vistas seem to go on forever.

I've carried that feeling indoors in the country interiors on the pages that follow, taking my inspiration from nature and adding those distinctive touches that could only come from the minds of men and women. You'll see studies in subtlety, to be sure, such as the collection I devised in collaboration with the great Italian designer Marella Agnelli, and exercises in outrageousness like the subtropical fantasy of Club Florida. There are interiors like Shibui that hew fairly closely to existing styles, and others—such as General MacArthur's Quarters—that celebrate a diversity of cultures.

Whatever the style might be, you can always count on finding some detail to astonish you or arrest your attention. That, in brief, is what *époustouflant* is all about.

Charleston-by-the-Sea

The gracious Southern coastal life epitomized by Charleston, South Carolina, inspired this Trend House, which combines with eloquence and grandeur elements of the old plantations and of seafaring to England and the Orient. On this verandah—an institution of the Old South—I placed twig chairs that were made for me by Amish craftspeople in Pennsylvania. The mermaid lamps are copies of ship figureheads.

What's a seaside house without a tele-
scope? This antique English one could
well have been brought to Charleston by
a ship's captain. England was also the
source of those fabulous bronze candelabra—elegant interpretations of flowers—
which date from the early to middle
nineteenth century. The china cabinets
(Charleston traders brought back beautiful porcelains from Asia) are reproductions from Baker Furniture's Charleston
Collection of original local pieces. Form-
ing a subtle background to the opulent
setting is a floor covering of cocoa matting, topped by Oriental area rugs that
dramatically define the spaces; the walls
are alternating bands of wood and drywall, covered in semigloss and flat paint;
and ceiling fans, suspended against a
gridwork of beams, stir the air.

Just as a pyramid is designed to draw the eye upward from its broad base to its apex, I designed this great room in such a way that the eye is drawn from the broad and luxurious sofas and armchairs, upholstered in velvet and moiré, toward the intriguing display perched high atop the mantel: a pair of old ship's lamps and, standing beside them, an antique dressmaker's dummy. Several more similar dummies stand beguilingly at that end of the room, like inscrutable guests at a party. Above the antique cabinet and period portraits, a pair of sculling oars emphasizes both Charleston's waterborne heritage and, more subtly, the proportions of the room.

In the study, the wall treatment of alternating semigloss- and flat-painted bands of wood and drywall forms a clean, crisp background that shows off the beauty of Baker's reproduction Charleston furniture. The blue-and-white Canton ware adds to the opulent, elegant theatrical air.

So many people lock away that wonderful crocheted-lace tablecloth they inherited from Grandmother, afraid it will get stained with food or red wine. I say, use it, with imagination! In this master bedroom, I didn't want the stifling feeling of a canopy, so I just draped Grandma's tablecloth diagonally across the top of the frame. The dynamic angular lines it creates, along with those of the Oriental rug, reduce the domineering scale of a big bed in a small room. Some old Louis Vuitton trunks and a pair of antique English oils add their own flavor of the stylish past.

English pencil post beds have a spare elegance that is complemented gorgeously with very simple bedmakings—down comforters covered in white cotton, with a woven blanket folded at the foot of each bed in case the night grows especially chilly. I found the botanical prints in England, and had them framed very plainly so that they wouldn't compete with the beds. The long, runner-like rug by the foot of the beds is an antique Persian whose subtle pattern doesn't attract too much attention, while the brass hardware on the chests of drawers at the far end of the room just knocks me out.

As an interesting variation on my Charleston-by-the-Sea house, I later took one of the rooms and—without changing the architecture, the wall treatments, or the cocoa matting—gave it an entirely new look, still Charleston in style, with different furniture arranged in a different way. The floral fabric on the sofas—a print from Baker's Charleston collection—joins with two Oriental ginger jars and other decorative items to give the room a more outgoing, lively air.

Wicker by Lauren

In another classic seaside variation, I started with a setting of rough-sawn cedar floor and walls to showcase wicker furniture from Ralph Lauren. Emphasizing the theme are framed old prints of shells and ornate pieces of coral atop an antique steel fireplace, from which oversized, handcarved wooden seashells tumble. A steel-and-brass hanging lantern works beautifully in this small room.

Log Cabin Eleganza

Our love of country style doesn't necessarily mean that we have to sacrifice elegance to rusticity. Take this cozy cabin, for example. I had the interior log walls lacquered in white, which adds a definite feeling of refinement. To enhance this elegant country look, I used a steel sleigh bed casually draped with handmade quilts; covered the floor with a brightly colored rag rug made for me in India; and upholstered the two comfortable lounging chairs in white cotton duck. Decorative touches, like the Italian clay pigs, the wonderful Vicenza stone sculpture, and the floral quilted pillows, create an interplay of rusticity and urbane sophistication. And, of course, there's that fabulous German armoire with its handpainted doors—the perfect embodiment of simplicity and elegance.

Country Pied-à-Terre

Though I originally developed this look with a small, sophisticated city apartment in mind, it's actually perfect for the kind of cozy country weekend residence popular with city people. In the bedroom, mattress ticking, used for the upholstery and the curtains, feels at the same time both casual and elegant. Complementing that feeling are a sleigh bed with down comforter and, from Interior Crafts, two French bergère chairs and a steel table. Introducing a contemporary touch is a standing neon lamp from Kovacs.

The living room of the Country Pied-à-Terre features an Italian hand-carved pine fireplace and two magnificent pine doors that I found in England. Over the mantel is a Venetian-style French mirror that has almost the feeling of a heraldic shield, lending the room an extra touch of elegance. Yet the overall look still is very soft and pretty.

Plywood House

With my love of textures, I was intrigued by the possibilities of plywood. The walls, columns, floors, and ceilings of this house are completely sheathed in that material, which has been repeatedly sanded and lacquered until it has a glasslike, almost mirrored finish. It's like living inside a boat, just slick and wonderful!

To contrast with the plywood's color and texture, I chose natural silk upholstery and silk rag rugs dyed in rich, vivid hues. Combined with such other items as plexiglass furniture, cat benches, oversized round-framed mirrors, an antique armoire, and track lighting, the atmosphere feels very contemporary, classic, and casual.

Italian Log Barn

I used the rough cedar log, one of my favorite looks, in a most unusual setting here, combining its rustic touch with marvelous open spaces and a mélange of furniture and vividly colored accessories to create an Italian Log Barn. The living area shown at left brings together the texture of a stucco fireplace, oversized floor tiles in black and white, geometric white sofas, and a magnificent hand-carved pine eagle from Florence, Italy. For the room's entryway, I installed stained-glass doors that I purchased from a confectionery shop in Paris.

An informal sitting room adjacent to the Italian Log Barn's dining area features hand-carved wooden sofas from Italy, and a custom carpet that visually ties into the checkerboard floor tiles while giving the room a shot of dazzling color.

The dining area is almost a soft loft concept. Note again the way I've combined a number of very basic components in an eyecatchingly strong mix— the pattern of the floor tiles, the textures of terra cotta, pine, cedar, and stucco— that once again illustrates that rules can indeed be broken!

The kitchen of the Italian Log House has led people to ask, "Well, who would put a crystal chandelier in their kitchen?" To which I reply, "If you can afford an antique Baccarat crystal chandelier, you can afford the servants to take care of cleaning it for you!" I designed this as a circular room. The sweep of Eurostyle cabinets mounted on the cedar walls embraces the country-style table that does triple duty as a work surface, dining area, and buffet, as well as a small sitting area with two comfortable chairs whose design is based on chairs aboard the French ocean liner *Normandie*.

In the bedroom, I chose cast-iron twig beds whose form echoes the cedar log theme; the bedding, like the upholstery throughout the house, is white on white. Take special note of the antique kilim carpets, which contrast with the checker board floor tiles for a wonderfully dramatic effect.

The Turquoise Room

Here's a dramatic example of how you can break up one very large space into several smaller rooms-within-a-room. The floor of this entire spacious area is covered in a rich turquoise carpet, which helps to tie the space together visually. But then I've carved it into several much more manageable areas by combining groupings of furniture and large Oriental carpets: a dining area with formal table and an ornately framed mirror above the sideboard; a small sitting room featuring a turquoise leather loveseat in the Chesterfield style; and a living "room" with two comfortable sofas in a lively floral print.

Italian Villa

Comfort is the underlying theme of this sitting room from an Italian Villa, in which the textural interplay of stucco walls, woven grass-mat-upholstered chairs, and velvet-textured Oriental carpets over terra-cotta floors makes the predominant visual statement.

I created a sort of directoire feeling with the furnishings in the Italian Villa's bedroom. Yet the point worth noting here is the way in which I boldly play against that feeling with the two-foot-square grey-green and white floor tiles and the wallcovering of barn siding—actually taken from an old barn that I bought and had torn down.

English Gothic

The oversized grandeur of a typical English hunting lodge was the inspiration for this opulent interior, which features the deep, rich burgundy colors I love so much. In the master bedroom, the burgundy walls and the same color in the Oriental carpet complement the deep brown woods of the oversized bed, the wardrobe, and the beamed ceiling. Among the country touches are an antler chandelier, oil portraits of thoroughbreds, and, mounted over the bed, a pair of castiron horse's heads from France.

In the lodge's dining room, the lush contrasts of burgundy and brown wood again set the tone. I particularly like the brass-and-glass hanging lamps and, hung on the wall on either side of the enormous china cabinet, a pair of old wine casks used as vases to hold dramatic sprays of dried branches.

Bavarian House

The inspiration for this house—a hunting lodge, really—comes from my many travels through Germany, where I'm always impressed by the masculine elegance of style and color. Yet I designed the furniture used here as a very contemporary line for Thayer Coggin in High Point, North Carolina, so I was eager to try it in this particular period setting.

In my usual way, I wound up liberally mixing a number of different styles in the Bavarian House: Bavarian, of course, along with English, Italian, French, and American. The antlers over the living room hearth come from the Black Forest, and the gold-leafed falcons were hand-carved for me in Italy. The iron and wood tables I found in France, and I had the wonderful chandelier made domestically to go with it all. The inspiration for the wall treatment of mahogany boards and plaster came from a building I admire in Verona. And what can I say? Anything that knocks you out is okay!

Though Italian in style, the dining table and chairs were made in America by Interior Crafts—and they go perfectly well with the Bavarian theme. I found the antlers for the chandelier in Austria and had them assembled in Chicago. The nickel-plated silver ram's dish, from Italy, is designed for serving enormous joints of roast meat—a real German-style banquet—and it goes beautifully with the pewter candlesticks on the sideboard in front of an old French tapestry. And I've provided a background of one of my favorite colors with a *sang-de-boeuf* carpet that matches the deep maroon color of the candles, and the oversized custom porcelain jars—which I brought in from Thailand!

The hunting lodge ambience of the Bavarian House comes through loud and clear in the den, which is very rich and masculine—from the *sang-de-boeuf* trunks and the furniture upholstered in deep maroon to the bearskin rug on the floor and the antlers mounted on the walls.

In the Bavarian House's guest quarters, a sense of Old World grandeur is summoned by the twin hand-painted pine wall beds, which I found in a house in Copenhagen. Continuing the hunting theme, the pair of white sateen-covered chairs I selected—from the Stately Homes of England Collection—have carved wooden lion's heads on their arms and lion's paws on their legs. In the background you'll see what is perhaps the only truly Bavarian piece in the room: an ornately handcarved chest.

In another effort at Bavarian style, I created this single room—which may be used as a home office or study—filled with far-flung items that, together, somehow capture that strong, stately German air. Worth noting are the heavily plastered walls, whose rough texture simulates plaster over stone; the Italian pottery; and the mahogany desk and the cane chairs from Italy.

Marella Agnelli Collection

I created the interior on the right after working on the Romantica fabric collection with the great Marella Agnelli. The fabrics are perfectly named—a wonderfully romantic floral pattern and coordinated stripe of soft pastel pinks, beiges, ivories, and greens. I used the floral fabric to upholster an Italian steel daybed, and the striped pattern to tie it together with a pair of comfortable armchairs. Note how the heavily stuccoed walls pick up the pastel pink, while the curve of the vaulted ceiling is repeated in the chairs and in the terra-cotta urns and Murano glass vase. By way of dramatic contrast to all that softness, I added a steel table and chairs and a stainless-steel-and-brass stove. Note how the dynamics I've set up in this relatively small, enclosed space capture the same feeling as the Italian villa terrace shown at left.

Alpine Ski Lodge

For Christmas one year, I was inspired
to create this ski lodge in a lighthearted
German Alpine spirit—an example of
painstaking attention to detail, since I
used, for the most part, only Bavarian or
German furniture. The wonderful pine
table and chairs are all from Germany,
as is the bed and the painted armoire.
To emphasize the colors of the season,
I added, of course, pots of poinsettias,
which play off the colors of the lap rugs
draped across the bed.

Looking in the opposite direction, you can see two American exceptions in this room: the yellow upholstered sofas I designed as part of my Jewel Collection. Their color plays well off the natural pine beams, and their bold geometric lines contrast nicely with the ornate German cuckoo clock on the far wall. Presiding over the whole scene—and keeping guard over the holiday presents piled on the table—is a fabulous sculpture I found in Paris. Remember: Go for anything that knocks you out!

High Country West

The collection I call High Country
West found its roots in my love of Native
American crafts and lore and in the
many trips I've taken to Santa Fe, New
Mexico, and to Cody, Wyoming, where
I worked with the Buffalo Bill Museum.
I enjoyed developing a log cabin concept
with some unusual flair—a basic, eighteenth-century dwelling with a wealth of
traditional and contemporary Western
touches that add up to what you might
call a "High Country attitude." To create
the walls, I had logs split so we could use
both sides, and applied them to a rough
plaster backing for the rustic ambience
I was after.

Handcrafted terra-cotta pottery, tremendous flowers and cacti, and a potpourri
of vivid colors on the beams, upholstery,
and accessories combine in the multi-
colored effect so prominent in nature's art—
particularly in the West and Southwest. To
finalize the concept, I chose pieces from
Baker Furniture's outstanding Charleston
Collection, but I directed Baker's North
Carolina craftspeople to upholster
the furniture in Pendleton Indian blankets.
The results absolutely knocked me out,
dramatically daring to be different. In
short: *époustouflant*!

The entry hall to High Country West sets the theme immediately with its use of a steer hide as a covering for the plain cedar floor. Beyond it, you see a wonderful pine burro that I found in England, of all places! Just like one of those animals people sometimes put in the rear windows of their cars, his head bobs up and down. I was so delighted when I saw him that I bought him then and there, long before I had conceived this room or had any idea that he might be a part of it.

Why shouldn't the kitchen be an art gallery too? This High Country West kitchen includes, above the sink, a work by noted Arizona artist R.C. Gorman as naturally as it includes strings of garlic hanging from the ceiling beams. The pine farm table and the Pendleton-covered Windsor chairs make this kitchen, for me,

a place to read, write letters, pay bills— just go about the business of daily life—as much as it is a place to sit down and enjoy a meal. Note also how much red predominates in this interior, even on the lampshades of the brass chandelier, while I chose black as the color for the kitchen appliances.

A vaulted ceiling gives the High Country master bedroom an especially spacious feeling. Once again, I've made liberal use of the brightly colored Pendleton fabrics, and a steer hide on the floor makes its own Western statement. Yet there's also a pencil post bed from the Charleston collection, along with Amish twig chairs and antique Louis Vuitton trunks that I brought in from England. All of these non-Western pieces nevertheless contribute to the overall feeling I was trying to achieve: a wonderfully warm, inviting environment.

The dining room makes the High Country West statement on the grandest scale of all, I think, and shows that pieces from many different lands can combine to create a unified look. Of course, there are the Pendleton blankets again, used to upholster the armchairs and as curtains hung from heavy pine rings. The animal skulls on the far wall were actually made for me by a Chicago artist, though you'll find decorated, sunbleached skulls like this throughout the West. The huge, ornately framed mirror on the right-hand wall came from Spain. And, believe it or not, those brass reindeer standing in the middle of the dining table came from Bangkok.

Santa Fe Lounging Bathroom

In a Southwestern spirit akin to my High Country West collection, I designed this Santa Fe lounging bathroom, which features Kohler fixtures, a whirlpool tub big enough for two, and—for relaxing after the bath—lodgepole beds with mattress ticking supported by crisscrossed rawhide straps. The stucco walls are stepped, in the architectural style you see throughout the Southwest, particularly in New Mexico. I found the handcarved wooden Indian in front of an old store out West. Take special note of the rocking chair, with its Kachina doll design.

Mexican Festival

With Mexican rugs and fabrics, Mexican
pottery, Mexican handmade wooden furniture, and a Mexican luncheon being
served, this setting looks and feels like
a fiesta. The love seat is an authentic
Mexican Victorian piece, which adds to
the feeling of old-fashioned romance and
imitates the curves of the vaulted ceiling
indigenous to the region. The fabrics in
this particular environment were hand-
woven exclusively for me by a lady from
Brooklyn who has worked for more than
two decades with Indian women, teach-
ing them to weave bright cottons such as
these; I had a special skirt made from
them as a wall piece. Altogether, the
intense colors create an exciting feeling
of *époustouflant*.

Chili Con Carne

Another Mexican variation, this room again features the saturated neon colors of exclusive hand-woven native fabrics. This time, I've carried those colors onto the walls, and added curtains to the arched windows in the same cotton that upholsters the metal frame chairs. I even prepared the menu myself, presenting the food in gaily covered baskets. The large cacti add a welcome contrast of deep green, not to mention a sense of desert drama.

Here's the basement recreation or family room, combined with a wine cellar, from my Mexican Festival collection. I've kept things a trifle more subdued here, picking up the bright colors from upstairs only in the red canvas of the classic director's chairs—which play wonderfully off the red necks of some of the bottles racked on the wall nearby. The Mexican theme continues more subtly in the black Oaxacan pottery, the terra-cotta, and the steer hide on the floor. One of the major pieces in the room is a bolero-type saddle—a beautiful example of Mexican leathercraft—which I put on special display simple by placing it atop a regular workshop-type sawhorse.

Irish Ways

By way of contrast to the intense liveliness of the Mexican Festival you've just been looking at, I thought it would be interesting to see a room in much more reserved, classic tones. The message here is the power of black to open up a room. Many people are afraid to use that color in their homes yet, as you can see, the black walls here actually expand a relatively small space. I use it quite a bit. I've picked up the black in the ticking stripes on the comforter and pillows, and in the leather upholstered chair.

61

Souleiado Collection

In recent years, I've had the great pleasure and honor of working with the Norman Demery family, whose company, Souleiado, in Terrasson near Avignon, France, manufactures exceptional fabrics in the French provincial style. In their honor, I styled a complete house—a country French chateau—in Souleiado fabrics. Our first glimpse of the interior is from the balcony, with antique iron balustrade, looking into the study. The room is composed of a lot of different elements from different places: a French pine fireplace surmounted by two African gazelle heads; a kilim rug on terra-cotta tiles; a beautiful steer-head sculpture with brass horns, from Florence; a marvelous steel-and-brass French baker's rack, filled with plants; terra-cotta parrots on pine occasional tables; antique French ceiling fixtures. What pulls them all together is the selection of bright, lively Souleiado fabrics.

The guest bedroom features a French sleigh bed and an antique love seat, both covered in a Souleiado fabric that was done exclusively for me to use in this room. Also worth noting are the Impressionist-style paintings, the antique iron furniture, and, at the far end of the room, one of the gracefully shaped wooden screens on casters which are used throughout the house in place of draperies.

In the living room of the Souleiado house, the bright pattern on the kilim rug complements yet another lively pattern from the fabric collection; its color, in turn, is picked up by the exuberant bouquet of roses, the perfect floral touch from Jason Spahn, who does all my flowers. I found the oversized brass candle sconces in France. They seem to me just the right scale for the generous vaulted ceiling.

Creating *époustouflant* in the dining room are old French wine baskets, which I've used as overscaled, wall-mounted vases for displays of hydrangeas. The walls here, once again, are decorated with paintings done in the style of Monet. Pine doors, made for me in Spain, lead to the adjoining living room.

The oversized host and hostess chairs at the two ends of the table are upholstered in black, which goes nicely with a black-ground Souleiado print on the other chairs in the room. Showering the dining table with light is an old billiard-table lamp.

I used various shades of red to bring
a feeling of warm intimacy to the
Souleiado master bedroom. Red paint
covers the steel frame of the bed canopy,
and the eight-inch floorboards, and a red
Souleiado print upholsters the love seat.
The mirror is a French version of a
Venetian-style frame, and beneath it is a
dresser from Baker. Some of the details I
especially like are the antique French
fireplace flanked by small topiary trees,
and the pine columns that seem to support the room at its four corners.

Giverny House

Having had the rare opportunity to work
with the Giverny Foundation at the home
of Claude Monet, outside of Paris, I created this gazebo-style presentation that,
I think, captures the spirit of the great
painter's famous, lovingly tended gar-
dens. Flowers, of course, are the main
theme: in the Giverny fabric for the love
seats, in the vivid fuchsia chintz upholstery for the chairs, in the Chinese floral
rug, and in the entire, sunshine-bright
yellow trellised structure that embraces
them. The handpainted Giverny screens
were created for me by artist Larry Coke.

French Country Barn

If you turn a few pages back to my High Country West collection, you'll see some strong similarities to the architectural structure I'm working with here. The point is, if you duplicate a scene while using different fabrics and different furniture design, you can create a whole new look—in this case, French Country. That style is announced here with the simplicity of a grey-green canvas awning and glimpses, through the divided-light windows, of a French provincial pattern more subdued than the Pendleton blankets I used to evoke the American West. A crystal chandelier certainly helps to place the house on the Continent. And that big old stuffed grizzly somehow manages to emphasize the country setting without really evoking a sense of the New World.

The dining room of my French Country Barn shows off a number of pieces from Baker's furniture collection known as French à la Carte. A lot of the pieces, such as the sideboard, are painted in charming country style. The very plain, heavy pine mantel—almost like a piece of butcherblock—seems in keeping with the split-log-and-plaster walls; backed by a simple mirror, it makes a wonderful display space for creating a sense of *époustouflant*. Note the arrangement of pumpkins and candlesticks, which adds to the rustic-yet-elegant air.

These guest quarters feature an elegant sleigh bed from Baker's French à la Carte, set at an angle to contrast with the structure's strong parallel, horizontal lines. Once more, in my usual spirit of breaking the rules and mixing styles, I've added the eyecatching touches of zebra-striped carpeting and a Southwestern steer skull, mounted above the window and on the far wall of the room.

71

In this master bedroom for the French Country Barn, I've used a French wrought-iron four-poster. To contrast with the dark iron, I selected very light wooden furniture, and I used a blue-and-white-striped floral fabric to cover the comforter, some throw pillows, and one of the chaises. The other two chaises are upholstered in cream-colored, quilted fabric. Take special note of the chevron-patterned kilim carpet, which—set against the natural wood floorboards—helps to tie the room together.

American Barn

I call this Trend House "American Barn" for a number of reasons. First, there's the architectural skin—corrugated metal roof, the beams, the mullion, the front and back structures—which is reminiscent of contemporary, industrial-style farm construction. Then there's the furniture—my design, manufactured exclusively for me by Interior Crafts—which is pure American Gothic. In many ways, the house is a study in the absence of color—there's just white, black, and shades of grey.

This interior view of the living/dining room offers a better look at the furniture's Gothic lines, and an even stronger sense of the barn's cathedral ceiling. The pale white, handcrafted ship makes, I find, an ethereal centerpiece for the dining table. As for the sphinx-like sculptures of women's heads, I had them custom made out of fiberglass for this environment. Remember: It's *époustouflant*, anything that will knock you out.

The bedroom of the American Barn is a marvelous study in grey and white. The queen-size bed's bamboo-shaped posts were cast in fiberglass; the tree-shaped lamps beside the bed are iron, with white patent-leather shades. I've used white chintz fabric throughout the room—take special note of the reverse canopy—and have given the entire setting a background of dark-grey stone floor and grey walls. The large, mottled Greek olive pot was, like everything else, expressly selected for this room.

I think this is the ultimate children's room. Not only is it full of wonderful toys, but the bed's headboard and footboard are beautiful, life-sized, hand-stuffed toy deers that I bought in Germany. Two antique benches on either side of the toy-town layout give children plenty of room for playing. One of my favorite features is the full electric train set that runs overhead on a plexiglass platform resting on the beams. It's the room we all would have loved to have had when we were growing up.

In the library, I've introduced a few flashes of color, particularly turquoise, into the grey-and-white scheme. All the contemporary upholstered furniture is, again, my design. The ceramic stove was imported from Italy, and I've eclectically added a pair of wooden Windsor chairs.

Club Florida

The subtropical exuberance of Florida is exemplified in this comfortable, vaulted space. You can have a lot of fun picking out the Floridian details. Of course, there are plenty of living plants, and a playful assortment of fake ones, including the torchère with its leafy fiberglass shade in the entry hall, and three different illuminated soft sculptural lamps that resemble oversized, ultra-exotic flora. There are several different oil paintings of flamingos and, above the doorway leading from the entry hall, a grinning ceramic crocodile head. A terra-cotta tile floor keeps things cool underfoot when the weather grows sultry.

These views of Club Florida offer a good chance to study the large, comfortably upholstered chairs, chaises, and sofas I selected from the Thayer Coggin Collection. In keeping with the subtropical theme, I've placed life-sized, almost-lifelike sculptures of game fish on the walls; there's a real fish swimming in the oversized globe fishbowl resting on its own pedestal. You'll notice, too, how elegantly different kinds of chandeliers adapt themselves to the graceful, spacious vaulted ceilings.

The master bedroom in Club Florida is relatively subdued, with a queen-sized bed upholstered in black, and a black chair in a contemporary design. The only tropical touches are the playful curtain fabric, draped around a giant plaster seahorse, and an assortment of tropical plants, including a flowering bromeliad to the right of the bed.

By way of contrast, the formal dining room is the most exuberant Club Florida setting of all. The eye immediately goes to the lively, colorful pattern of tropical leaves and flowers, which repeats on the fireplace tiles, the columns at the room's corners, and alternating oversized tile squares. A foliage design repeats just as brashly in the design of the dining chairs by Niedermaier, and more subtly on the ceiling molding and the picture frames for the spectacular paintings by Deborah Daly. Of course, there's another pretend croc head above the fireplace.

Palm Beach Collection

To me, Palm Beach evokes many images and feelings: spaciousness, elegance, grandeur, ultra-chic style. Money is no object here. This brick-floored promenade leading to the main entrance of my Palm Beach house is flanked by palm trees lit at angles from below and above to highlight the delicate, breezy form of their fronds.

Inside, the entry hall is guarded by twin stone lions that I had carved for this setting in Vicenza, Italy. Beside them are shallow pools, romantically lit at night with floating candles. The sand-colored decking allows an outdoors feeling to flow into the room.

In the decked dining area, I've set up three small tables—which, I think, creates a more exciting atmosphere than just one large table for all the guests. Plates and vases of Murano glass introduce bright subtropical colors. The wicker chairs, combined with the deck-style flooring and the tall palm trees, help to conjure the feeling that you're dining outdoors, while the enormous crystal chandelier of Italian cut glass is the height of indoor elegance. I've also opted for elegant draperies over the French doors.

Cool, casual elegance reigns in the Palm Beach living room. The colors are white, white, white, offset by the green awning stripe on the sofa, the deep green carpeting, the wonderful pastel colors of Murano glass candlesticks on the mantel, and the exuberant floral display. The chairs flanking the fireplace were originally designed by Angelo Donghia. I had the stone figures representing the four seasons—you see two of them by the fireplace, one by the far window— carved for me in Vicenza, Italy.

Of course the sitting room/study of the Palm Beach house would include a wonderful atrium filled with tropical plants. In their midst is a piece of statuary, a copy of Michelangelo's David. The white-upholstered chaise offers the ideal place to lounge in the afternoon; the furniture is a mixture of antiques and pieces from the Interior Crafts collection.

The master bedroom, seen here in two different views, is definitely *époustouflant*. At the bed's four corners are four sinuous, enormous columns, each holding a planter with an exuberance of tropical foliage. Handcarved wooden shells decorate the fireplace. An ornate, oversized Venetian mirror dominates one wall. Yet none of the astonishment happens at the expense of comfort. The French sofa from Interior Crafts, the stacks of pillows—everything is welcoming and cozy amidst the overall enormous scale.

Shibui Collection

"*Shibui*"—it means "the ultimate in beauty" to the Japanese. During numerous trips to Japan, I have always been impressed by the purity of the Japanese line, its minimalism and tranquility. But I wanted to do my own thing with it, my own interpretation of its refined, restrained, classical style. Thus my Shibui Collection was born, and I think it captures in a unique way the authentic country simplicity of Japanese living. The materials are exquisitely natural and perfectly crafted: the handcarved stone garden lantern and water stone, both bought by me in Japan; the sliding window screens, made there to my specifications; the rustic bamboo bench; and the carefully raked gravel, like a moat surrounding the house.

The design concept in my Shibui Collection is totally Japanese, with a few adaptations for the way we Westerners live. In the dining room shown on the left, for example, the cushions at the extra-long table are mounted on casters so that Americans who have a difficult time sitting on the floor can be a little more comfortable. In the master bedroom shown below, the classic butterfly chairs, done in black leather, are a fine example of how well new styles can mix with the old; I designed the angular Japanese-style table as part of the collection. Likewise for the furnishings in the main living room at right, which is a truly beautiful example of the principle that less is more. The pine beam ceilings, tatami mats, and shoji screens are constant, classical elements in all three rooms.

In this Asian variation, I've combined Japanese and Chinese influences in peaceful harmony. The sofas from Thayer Coggin are covered in a rich, deep violet cotton sateen that I find very exotic. I found the beautiful altar table in China, and the handcarved capitols atop the lacquered columns come from Taiwan. The two matching floral arrangements are wonderfully spare, very Asian.

The rooms shown on this page represent very different Asian approaches. The room shown on the right, which could be a small living room or study, places an emphasis on the exotic, with deep red walls, a sofa upholstered in a dynamic Japanese print called Itamaki, which I designed, and a touch at once contemporary and traditional: an oversized, paper-sculpture doll of a Japanese guard in authentic dress. Yet backing up all this drama are simple tatami mats on the floor. In the photograph below, you see a more thoroughly traditional Japanese environment I created, which serves as both bedroom and sitting room, complete with tatami mats and shoji screens. It's serene, quiet, and very elegant.

The Japanese bath is a truly serene ritual, and I paid serious attention to it in my Shibui Collection. I had a master craftsman from the mountains build for me an authentic water-bearing wooden bathtub; the wood expands when wet, so there's absolutely no leakage. At the ready are a small bathing stool, a water bucket for rinsing, and separate stations with plush white towels for Mama, Papa, and the children. The red walls heighten the sense of drama, and I added the Chinese gong purely for decoration and for its size. A single orchid twines perfectly around an upright bamboo pole, like a Japanese *haiku* poem.

General MacArthur's Quarters

General Douglas MacArthur made his World War II headquarters in the Manila Hotel. I visited that hotel, and got permission to reproduce the wicker furniture from his suite—manufactured for me by White Craft. Wicker aside, the photos you see here don't look anything like the rooms MacArthur really occupied; they're my *époustouflant* interpretation of the kind of quarters he *should* have lived in: heroic, colorful, exotic, and masculine.

To capture the exotic air here, I used sisal carpeting and had the walls and ceiling covered with woven Philippine basket material, and the baseboards, door frames, columns, and beams with bamboo poles. The mahogany furniture pieces are from the Philippines, the small wooden elephant table from Bangkok, while the fabrics range from Asian carpets to zebra-patterned upholstery to Scottish plaid cushion covers. To evoke MacArthur's heroism, I combed history books for images from his entire military career, starting with West Point, then had my stable of artists in New York convert them into portraits of epic proportion.

The Crown and the Eagle

When *this* American designer does an English country house, overscale is definitely the key. Enormous, twelve-foot-tall columns herald the entrance— massive double doors made for me in Italy—to the house I call "The Crown and the Eagle." The hanging porch fixture was imported from France. In the English country style, plants abound, both alongside the entrance pathway and on a wonderful plant rack centered just inside the door.

If you want to create a truly grand environment, you don't hold yourself back, you go for it, one hundred percent. That's what I did in this living room. The chandelier is covered in 24-karat gold leaf—absolutely magnificent. The overscaled chairs are covered in rich suedes and hound's tooth patterns—I used Ralph Lauren fabrics—complemented by fabulous Oriental carpets. Of course, an environment such as this must have a grand piano.

The grand four-poster in the master bedroom of my English country house comes from the Baker's Stately Homes of England collection. Draped across the head of the bed is Versace mosquito netting in silk, which can be pulled down to afford the occupants just a little more privacy. Between a pair of love seats, one of them swathed in exotic furs, are two elephant's-foot cocktail tables upholstered with zebra. On a trip to London, I found the royal portraits, for which deep burgundy walls provide an appropriately rich background. And you can't miss the very key *époustouflant* element here: the stuffed African leaping lion, surely a prize bagged on an expedition into the far reaches of the Empire.

The dining room of my English country house is another regally overscaled composition. A beautiful Oriental carpet almost fills the room. Rich, stately furniture from Baker and a massive fireplace form the setting for a magnificent collection of blue-and-white Canton porcelains; on the mantel, they're backed with miniature ivy topiaries reminiscent of the larger, meticulously trained and trimmed plants one finds in a great English garden. Another feature I like about this room is the telescopic spotlighting—track lights that work like telescopes, enabling you to intensify or diminish individual beams of light wherever you'd like them.

It's a very British tradition for the men to retire after dinner to the game room, so just off the dining room I've created this gentlemen's setting which features a marvelous antique snooker table that I found at Keith Skeel's Antiques in London. I've blended the table into the deep green library-style room, with mahogany baseboards and floor, and Persian tapestries on the wall. One of the most interesting points about this room is the lighting: a rather Nouveau brass billiard lamp over the table and, by the window, a torchère to contribute just a touch of ambient illumination on the ceiling.

This small study contrasts a bright red Scottish plaid upholstery with those deep green walls and deeply polished hardwood floor. Again, note the emphasis on ambient lighting, used to deft effect at the small dining table, at the point where the two sofas meet, and on the plant and various *objets.*

Casa de Campo

Many people are intrigued by the.thought of what an interior designer's own home might look like. As you can see, in mine, I've combined a lot of the different country-style elements that have appeared on the previous pages. With my penchant for contrasting styles to achieve a sense of *époustouflant*, my living room is filled with intriguing visual treats: a ceramic horse's head from England above the mantel; a deep burgundy sofa whose color is picked up by the flowers in the large fishbowl vase; informal-looking wicker chairs challenging the high formality of the grand piano; the ornate Oriental carpet against the simplicity of terra-cotta tiles.

My eclecticism continues to express itself in the guest bedroom. Note how the walls—a rich, warm brown color—display a sun-bleached Southwestern steer skull, a primitive African woodcarving, and a German poster. The wood-and-brass ceiling fan, the wicker bed with its safari plaid comforter and pillow cases, the bentwood rocker: all contribute to a feeling of coziness.

My bathroom, unlike some, is warm and welcoming rather than cold and clinical. The informality of the terra-cotta floor tiles makes for a nice contrast with the ornate, marble-topped vanity cabinet by Kohler, mahogany-framed mirror, and gilt sconces. The floor-to-ceiling mirrors in the shower make the space seem far larger. And the red plaid towels really liven things up.

Terra-cotta tiles not only cover the kitchen floor but also the counters—a fabulous look, and very easy to maintain. I've got enough counter space to be able to display some wonderful! antique crystal decanters—especially *époustouflant* in this relatively rustic setting—as well as a collection of ceramic Brazilian voodoo heads on the far buffet counter near the breakfast room.

I've created this as a real gentleman's study, with robust red plaids on the sofa, the chairs, and the cushions for the wicker love seat, a zebra skin on the floor, a deer head on the far wall, and various other masculine touches. With my love for over-sized touches, the hand-carved Spanish mirror, which I designed, is just fabulous here. And the Eiffel Tower French vase on a Plexiglass table really grabs the eye. Let me also, somewhat shyly, point out the small rhinoceros sculpture on the chest near the windows—it's a piece I did as an art student in college.

As an interior designer, it seems as if I don't show exteriors all that often. Well, this is the exterior of my own home, itself a pleasing mixture of the styles I like. You might call the architecture Spanish or Italian—call it Mediterranean. The trees and shrubbery provide the same kind of lush living setting as I try to bring to so many indoor environments. And what could be more country-style British than a pair of Airedales? Believe me, they are *époustouflant*!

En Ville

To far too many of us, city life conjures up images of a humdrum existence plagued by unrelieved confinement, noise, and pollution. I say there's only one solution to that state of affairs: Create your own haven in the city by fashioning a home environment that practices the principles of *époustouflant*.

You'll find plenty of examples to inspire you on the following pages. Take the Media House, which celebrates the modern age with an explosion of bright colors and high-tech equipment. Or my Blacks and Whites interior, in which I demonstrate the visual excitement that a stark palette can generate. In a more traditional vein, there's the ethereal serenity of my Vivere Italiano villa, which takes a lesson or two from centuries-old European interiors. And my Normandie Collection, which captures the elegance of ocean travel in its heyday.

Any one of these interiors—even a single idea out of a single room—would make a tremendous starting point for transforming your own city life. Or mix up a potpourri of different ideas. Eclecticism, after all, is a major element of *époustouflant*.

Sang-de-Boeuf

I love to work in deep, red-brown burgundy. It's a shade you sometimes see re-
ferred to as *sang-de-boeuf*—blood of the
ox—which is a term I find quite evoc-
ative. The color is rich and strong enough
to hold together this very large-scale setting full of emphatic objects—including
a stone fireplace featuring a stainless-
steel hood, a zebra skin on the floor,
stacks of antique leatherbound books,
and a wonderful old poster for some sort
of French elixir.

Deep burgundies work marvelously in a holiday environment such as this one, where an overall sense of festivity reigns—from the tree and the gaily wrapped packages to the antique coffee table made of antlers, the profusion of poinsettias to the red and gold obelisks in front of the gilt-framed English mirror, the handcarved Italian pine wall console to the wonderful old kilim pillows and the zebra-striped wool carpet from Stark.

In similarly opulent style, I designed this office/study/library for the great actor John Malkovich, who, as you may know, got his start with Chicago's Steppenwolf Theatre Company. For the desk, I used a gigantic, long oak table; the desk chair is a large-scale Bavarian antique that I found, and across from it are two chairs with lion's head arms from the Stately Homes of England collection. Antique Louis Vuitton trunks look just right beneath the old baronial gent in the oil portrait, who himself looks like he might later slip into that suit of armor. Believe it or not, there's also a small computer and a television set in the room.

To me, many of Ralph Lauren's fabrics capture that incredibly rich warmth of red-brown *sang-de-boeuf*. I've used a number of different fabrics from his collection in this living room: a paisley wallcovering above the mahogany wainscotting; a tapestry print on the sofa; a floral on the near armchair and a geometric on the far one. To complement it all, I chose a marvelous Oriental rug and added to the countryman's environment with stuffed animal heads and hunting prints.

Just to show that I'm not entirely wedded to blood-rich colors, let me present by way of contrast this study in grey and black. All the fabrics here are wool—the curtains, the upholstery, and the carpet with its small geometric pattern. The Venetian mirror's silvery tones and the grey of the steel China cabinet reinforce the color scheme, while I've introduced a vibrant touch with the Chinese rug and a flash of white light with that wonderful Japanese paper lamp behind the sofa.

Christian Lacroix Quarters

Long before I met the great French couturier Christian Lacroix, I delighted in his first collection, which featured straw hats with the flowers sticking out of the top. I decided to do a room based on them, to see if I could capture that feeling in a home furnishings environment. What we did was create what I call a planter mantel—like a sculptural window box set atop a mantel and illuminated with grow lights in the ceiling spots above. Popping out of that box are real growing garden flowers, with more arrayed around the base of the fireplace. I did the rest of the room in a warm white—almost like the color of a straw hat—and used an ivy-green fabric for the upholstery and a color-splattered painter's dropcloth as an area rug. The overall effect is fairly simple, but no less effective and beautiful.

After I got to know Christian Lacroix, we decided one year to design a Christmas room together, with an emphasis on the way he would enjoy his holiday in his villa in the South of France. The chairs I put together with Interior Crafts, called the Crown Jewels collection. We covered the walls from the chair rail to the floor with a marvelous *trompe l'oeil* French wallpaper; the top half of the walls, a dark navy blue, we adorned with hand-painted gold stars. On the floor are terracotta tiles with gold insets, and brightening the room are an antique French deco chandelier and an antique gold-leaf English mirror.

Northern Italian Collection

I designed my Northern Italian Collection for a two-apartment graystone building on Chicago's Astor Street. What I wanted was a lush, hushed, elegant look, featuring unusual one-of-a-kind accessories and color combinations. The color of the walls and the carpets is my invention, the result of seemingly endless experiments until I excitedly arrived at what I call BIV—which stands for blue-indigo-violet. It became the dominant factor here, along with subdued lighting that enhances this quiet environment and brings it into focus.

Throughout this collection, you'll see Baker Furniture's Northern Italian line—which, I think, conveys just the right air of subdued elegance. Another important element worth noting is the handcarved moldings covered in black lacquer and 24-karat gold leaf; I had them custom made in Barcelona for this apartment.

In the dining room, I had the chairs covered in a soft, mocha-brown fabric—which creates a soft shimmer of *époustouflant* against the BIV walls and drapes. The antique silver candelabra I bought in England to enhance this particular room, and the mirror—hand-carved with 24-karat gold leaf—comes from Spain. Terra-cotta planters from Italy add a slight country touch to this very city apartment.

This view of the den offers an excellent view of those black-lacquer-and-gold-leaf moldings around the doorway leading to the bedroom. The drapery treatments help to enhance, I think, an illusion of spaciousness. Note how the hawk's blood velvet on the armchairs both contrasts and complements the BIV. All the paintings in the room are antique English oils, and the bust in the background is ceramic with a faux marble finish, made for me in Italy.

An important facet of my Northern Italian concept involved carrying the motif throughout the house—even into the master bathroom you see here. Those one-of-a-kind contemporary artist vases along the top of the tub were found by me in France; I selected all the accessories, making sure that they're unique, unusual, and irreplaceable.

In this view of the Kohler bathroom, you see that it's a full European-style bath, including bidet. One important thing to point out here is the use of artwork and family photographs on the wall. We spend a lot of time in the bathroom, and it's nice to be able to look at such a specially framed collection.

Mark Hampton Collection

The second apartment at Astor Street is based on a furniture collection designed by Mark Hampton in a setting conceived by me. The furniture is styled very much in the spirit of the eighteenth and nineteenth centuries, with some wonderfully rich leather upholstery that is in perfect harmony with the period Oriental rug. I've used a bright red color on the walls, and you'll notice that I've kept the same custom moldings of black lacquer and gold leaf as in the other apartment.

The living room in this apartment includes a spacious, slowly rising stairway along one wall, leading to the living quarters on the second floor. For the sofa and one of the chairs, I chose a chintz fabric with a large floral print—a bold move in this room filled with oversized furnishings—which goes marvelously with the red walls, the heavy-beamed ceiling, and the antique English oils.

The other end of the living room nicely illustrates, I think, how you can pull all kinds of styles and periods together in one place. Look at the way in which the red walls, the brown carpets, and the cabana-strip upholstery help to bridge the gaps between eighteenth, nineteenth, and twentieth centuries.

Eighteenth-Century Tradition

In an interesting comparison to the Mark Hampton rooms, this setting was conceived by me as a very traditional eighteenth-century environment. There's lots of gold and black—on the mirror, moldings, and walls, on the marble floor, and in the especially strong statement made by the 24-karat gold-leaf chandelier. The striped silk fabric I chose for the upholstery is rich indeed, contributing to this room's wonderfully comfortable feeling.

Avant Premiere

To me, Avant Premiere means a thrilling collection of several different compatible styles: French, Italian, contemporary, nouveau — and especially deco, as embodied in the paintings I had done for this series of rooms in the style of the great Polish painter Tamara de Lempicka. In the den, seen here, the leather chairs were designed exclusively for this trend house by John Mascheroni; they proved so successful that they're now carried in the Swain line. The table was made at my request by the New York firm As If. The gilt-and-frosted-glass chandelier is French.

The dining room demonstrates one of my favorite practices: multiple tables and chairs, which create, I think, more excitement at a dinner party. If you wanted, of course, you could pull them together to make one big formal table. Both the fireplace and the chandeliers are French deco. As in the previous room, the tables and chairs are by, respectively, As If and John Mascheroni.

I based the design for the récamiers in this lounge on an old Italian one I saw. Maybe I should say *loosely* based, since I changed the legs and upholstered them in African zebra skins. As If in New York manufactured the glass-topped table with the steel and walnut legs at my request, as well as those simple, sinuous lamp stands with the flame bulbs, and the very dramatic silver-leaf fiberglass chair with black cushion, which was designed by Ventura. The chandelier, once more, is an old French nouveau design; the floor tiles are black and gold marble. And look how the effusion of gladioli picks up the military red in that Tamara-style portrait!

140

A small sunroom off the lounge in Avant Premiere features more black leather chairs and some very comfortable, cream-colored chaises. Note the very casual elegance in the way the drapes bunch on the floor. A simple Italian sconce provides ambient lighting in the alcove that shelters yet another oversized Italian deco painting.

In the master suite, I wanted nothing less than a fabulous, heroic bed with flames rising from its four posts. So I made a sketch of my idea, and the people at As If took it from there; I call it my Statue of Liberty bed. The columns are walnut, the flames gold leaf; the frame is made of

steel and optical glass. The ceramic vase at the foot of the bed was done in my favorite BIV—blue-indigo-violet. I refer to the fiberglass chairs covered in 24-karat gold leaf as Louis-Louis chairs; their seats and arms are upholstered in gold moiré.

143

Blacks and Whites

My love of zebra stripes was the starting point for designing this cool tropical-style city retreat. Very contemporary Italian black-and-white furniture combines here with two-foot-square black and white floor tiles, black-painted wicker, and zebra-patterned upholstery. To play up the jungle attitude, I added handcarved wooden animals. A pressed-tin ceiling—the sort you might find in old American or French grocery stores—keeps a cool lid on the place, and the white ceiling fan idly stirs the breeze. Don't you find the absence of color very refreshing?

In the fifties, black and white with red was a very popular combination, thanks in part to Christian Dior. Here I've used black and white, with a few red accents, in a very avant-garde, Eurostyle setting that I think also looks very Japanese. The furniture is contemporary Italian, the deck flooring horizontal stripes in black and white; look around the room and you'll see a huge variety of materials—iron, lacquer, Lucite, ceramic—all in black and white.

In this bedroom, black and white and shades of grey—faux-slate floor, a sleigh bed fully upholstered in ticking, cabana-striped pillows on the bed and the chaise—are accented with a splash of color from Murano glassware. Notice how the white and black somehow seem to bring out the grey undertones in the colors of the vases and candlesticks.

Media House

From the almost total absence of color in my Blacks and Whites collection, we move on to some really startling color combinations in my Media House. The whole idea behind this room was to juxtapose bright, wonderfully lively colors. I designed all the furniture—in simple, contemporary lines—which was manufactured for me by Interior Crafts. The media part of the concept enters into the picture here through a four-station video center: four separate TV monitors, each with separate sets of earphones leading to the four corner seating areas, so you can have four separate viewing parties going on at the same time. The top of the table is perfectly empty, so you can put snacks out buffet-style. The walls and floor, by the way, are done in *sang-de-boeuf*.

As part of the master suite, I've created the ultimate bathing environment. There's a shiny black marble bathing pool, from which you can enjoy the warm glow of a fire in the antique French art nouveau fireplace that I bought in Paris. Those wonderful chintz chaises are waterproofed, so you can relax there on your towel after the bath.

The sleeping quarters in Media House are just a touch more subdued than the big TV viewing room, with a bed—though it looks like a sofa—that I designed with Angelo Donghia. The upholstery is 100 percent woven wool scraps. As you can tell by the windows, this set of rooms would be wonderfully at home on the top floor of a vintage old city building. The white grand piano is for Bobby Short to play when he comes to visit, of course.

It seems that hand-in-hand with our media-obsessed society goes an obsession with high-tech physical fitness equipment, so Media House includes a fully equipped exercise room, complete with Universal weight machine. The entire concept is coordinated; the black leather workout benches, the white floor and ceiling, the silvery chrome of the equipment, and the bright red of the towels. You also get a good look here at the elegant vaults and archways, quite a change from this apartment's original flat, ten-foot ceilings.

Lycra Loft

The colors of the room you see on these two pages are in the same vivid spirit as the Media House. The walls, floor, and ceiling are chrome yellow, red, and violet; all the upholstery is stretchy Lycra—bathing suit material. All these elements are in keeping with the high-tech fun of a home gymnasium. Hence the white locker unit and, although you can't quite see it, a recessed whirl-pool bath on the upper level. The bright abstract paintings were done for me by local Chicago artists.

Normandie Collection

Though it is conceived as part of a house, I imagined this room as a multi-level lounge on the great luxury liner *Normandie*. The furniture is actual reproductions by Thayer Coggin from original chairs on board the ship. The bar centers on a huge stainless-steel column, and the wonderful stools are by Interior Crafts. The walls and ceiling are sheathed in matte stainless steel, which only makes the velvet of the upholstery and carpeting feel all the more plush.

Another room in the Normandie
Collection features oversized porthole
windows—a city apartment-sized
version of the far smaller portholes
you'd actually find on the liner.
Once again, there are Thayer Coggin's
Normandie-style chairs and sofa, with
a wonderful deco table.

The *Normandie*'s deco styling continues in this rather intimate dining room. I've opted here for soft pastel-pink uphol-stery to go with the cream-colored table base and buffet top. These colors look particularly delicate and appealing against the rich burgundy-brown of the walls and floor. Note how the dining table's round glass top echoes the shape of the portholes, and how the discreet touches of brass—the buffet base, the leaping fish on the table—serve to accent the feeling of opulence.

Lesage

The Monsieur Lesage with whom I did this glorious room was the grandson of the original Lesage who started the great Paris couture house known for the magnificent gold-and-jewel embroidery and beadwork it did for the likes of Chanel, Valentino, and Saint Laurent. My goal was to produce a room in the spirit of Lesage. Working with his exper-tise in embroidery, we created a pattern in 24-karat gold which we applied to the back of a rose moiré-upholstered antique French love seat with gilded wooden trim. I've just got to say that the seat retails for a mere $22,000. We used it with copies of Russian furniture from the French villas of Russians who escaped prior to the Communist Revo-lution. Everything else, of course, is trimmed in gold, à la Lesage: the chan-delier is 24-karat, and brass-plated rods and rings hold the black moiré wallcover-ing that drapes luxuriously to the floor.

Vivere Italiano

I like to think of this villa-like loft apartment as a study in magnificent simplicity. Just consider the elements that have gone into it. The columns and vaulted ceilings create a space almost reminiscent of a cathedral — the perfect setting for the awe-inspiring, five-by-ten-foot copies of Michelangelo's Sistine Chapel frescoes, produced on handmade paper by an unknown Italian artist and found in an old chapel in southern Italy. The floor is polished black travertine. I upholstered the sofas — which look like three-dimensional artworks in their own right — in the same kind of silver-grey silk that you find lining mink coats. One of the most stunning elements in this very *époustouflant* room is the Italian octagonal table of ivory and black lacquer.

The dining room has my usual multiple-table arrangement, featuring Interior Crafts' wonderful baroque Italian chairs—which I upholstered with a Marella Agnelli pattern—around navy blue lacquered Parsons tables. The vaulted ceiling is a perfect setting for the two Italian crystal chandeliers with brass fittings. In this subdued, elegant interior, the pair of azure Murano glass bowls are just electrifying.

Architecturally speaking, I find the placement of this lounging room particularly exciting. You can look to your right and see some of the Sistine Chapel artwork in the grand room, or look along the length of the elegantly vaulted and columned room toward a wall-sized window. The scale of the room makes it an

ideal space for displaying art, and the Angelo Donghia–designed chairs—which I had manufactured with Interior Crafts and covered in a high-polished cotton—have a sculptural impact as powerful in their way as the life-sized Vicenza stone figure.

Here's another take on Italian city living: a contemporary apartment with hand-carved walnut doors, leather upholstery, and a grand piano. I had the greyhound carpets made for me in Como. The light sculpture on the wall above the black-lacquered Italian buffet presents a constantly changing display of geometric shapes and colors.

This Italian garden room features a ceramic garden table from Florence, with handcarved leaf chairs. Apart from that, the room merely has a collection of Italian terra-cotta planters, resting on the black travertine floor. It's a good exercise in the powerful look you can sometimes achieve by not putting too much in a room.

Inexpensive City Opulence

I achieved this rather rich-feeling Oriental city apartment look at a fairly reasonable cost. The humped camel-back sofas, for example, are similar to ones I've used in other circumstances, but here they're covered in a less expensive fabric that still manages to have the look of a Mark Hampton. On the wall are Oriental clay paintings that I bought in New York. The pine furniture is all from my exclusive import collection from Spain and England.

Here's another fine example of a magnificent style that is achievable in the affordable price range. In this case, the furniture is upholstered in a Ralph Lauren–look fabric that is actually synthetic, not wool. The marble columns in the room are actually plaster, painted to look like marble. And by keeping costs down on most of your furnishings in this way, you can allow yourself to splurge on one really outrageously high-quality piece, like the campaign chest with brass base at the center of the room.

The Green House

What I was trying to do here was experiment with tradition, adding some of my own trademarks—over-sized pieces, eclectic accessories—to a well-established look. In this study, with its dining table–style reading desk, the green two-foot tile floor, the green curtains over the arched window, the green walls are all fairly standard concepts, but I've pushed them to their limits. As a visual pun, I've added a greenhouse ceiling. And you need the cream-colored upholstery—a rich crewel—to give you some relief from the intensity of color.

Of particular interest in this sitting room is the green-and-white welting I carried over from the curtain sashes to define the outline of the architectural space. It helps to, quite literally, tie the room together. The traditional saddle-brown leather sofa looks magnificent here.

To break up the fairly large expanse of the living/dining room in the Green House, I've placed a pair of zebra skins at odd angles on the floor. See how readily the eye is drawn to the display of china in the cabinets on the far wall? Just a few touches of white really stand out amidst all the rich green.

Working with the idea of the master bedroom as a retreat from the rest of the house, I've made a rich cream the dominant color here, on walls, ceiling, and curtains and upholstery; only the welting and the carpet tie the space visually to the rest of the house. The two chaises at the room's far end offer a setting that is both grand and comfortable.

Starting Points

Sometimes, one particular piece will set off a whole chain reaction of interior design ideas. The design for the room on the left began with that magnificent tiered antique Japanese vanity chest: Look at the beautiful iron work on that piece! Deco somehow feels very comfortable with the Japanese look, so I

added those red-and-yellow sculptural light columns at the room's corners, along with a simple dining table covered with a white quilted cloth and set with blue-and-white Canton ware. The yellow and red ball cushions on the wicker sofa and the ceramic Chinese Fu dog all contribute to the stylistic interplay.

The starting point for the room above was that huge, *époustouflant* abstract oil on the wall. I picked up the yellow from it for the walls and ceiling, and found compatible colors and similar patterns in the large Indian dhurrie on the floor. Note the antique sideboard, which I've actually placed so that it partially blocks a corner of the painting: another rule broken!

I've managed, I think, to achieve a simple country charm in a vaulted city space here. My eye keeps being drawn to that terra-cotta sphere in the middle of the table; the setting gives it an almost mystical quality. The Wedgwood blue walls, the window covering cut at its odd angle, and the rose and white painted floor all seem to focus the gaze right back to the center. But don't miss the display of blue-and-white Canton ware on the two tables that flank the windows.

My inspiration here was the marvelous Amish quilt; once I saw it, I knew I had to design a room around it. So strong is the quilt's pattern and colors that I felt it needed the neutral, simple color and texture of wicker furniture, but I picked up the plum color and used it on the cushions — not to mention the painted wood ceiling beams.

French Fantasy Dining

I went to a fabulous flea market in Paris to find all the elements of this fantastic dining environment; marble-topped bistro tables, bistro chairs, antique mirrors and lighting, and authentic bakery fixtures. To them, I added an American pressed-tin ceiling, green walls, and two-foot-square green and white floor tiles. Imagine creating such a dining fantasy for entertaining—the excitement generated when your guests mingle from table to bar to dessert display and back to table. *Comme on dit en Français, "C'est époustouflant!"*

Dossier

Shibui Shop

As part of my continuing fascination with things Japanese, I put together this elaborate display featuring many of the absolutely marvelous traditional and modern Japanese products we in the West have access to today. I made use of shoji screens to define the space, lined the display areas with tatami mats, and arrayed all manner of objects—from lacquer trays to woven placemats, paper lanterns to folk-art tigers, ceremonial armor to intricately woven silk robes. Quite a sensation was created!

Christmas, European-Style

If there was ever a time of year meant for giving free rein to fantasy, Christmas is it. That thought was the guiding spirit behind this holiday display, which I filled with every classic element of a European Christmas: old-fashioned gnome-like Santas and delicate Edwardian-style dolls, nutcrackers large and small, and tree ornaments of every description. Of course, there had to be a sleigh, and I couldn't resist filling it to overflowing with toy reindeer.

Focus: Scandinavia

In terms of contemporary design ideas, one of the world's most influential regions is Scandinavia. An in-store promotion for Scandinavian products led me to put together this environment, which gave emphasis to the primary colors so popular in that part of the world—and offered me the opportunity to assemble a whole battalion of painted toy soldiers.

Carnivale

The season of Carnival generally means letting yourself go with abandon. What better excuse could there be for an exercise in *époustouflant*? My associate Ron Fiori and I chose outrageous colors, eyecatching mannequins, energetic posters, and a bright-red horse as the background for a display of everything from beach chairs to dishware to high-flying kites—anything that encourages you to let yourself go!

Field's Afar

In creating this Marshall Field's shop offering "Distinctive Gifts for the Gentleman," I made a bordeaux red 1936 Allard sports roadster — bought at Christie's auto auction in London — the centerpiece that went miles in evoking the sense of ultimate quality we wanted to convey about a shop selling everything from fine antique oil paintings to classic cufflinks.

Formal Black and Cafe Noir

My love for basic black and white led me, with the help of my associate Ron Fiori, to come up with this exquisite Formal Black shop and its adjoining cafe, called—naturally enough—Cafe Noir. As you can see, in the shop we offered everything from classic crystal to black leather furniture. The cafe, replete with chairs upholstered in zebra-patterned fabric, presented the weary shopper with a selection ranging from croissants and hot tea or chocolate to caviar and iced Stolichnaya vodka.

French Quarters and French Barn

In a similar spirit to Formal Black and Cafe Noir, we created the French Quarters environment, combining a country bistro atmosphere with an appealing collection of French provincial items, from basketry to pottery to Pierre Deux prints.

The World's Finest

I feel very fortunate to have the opportunity through my job to work with the world's most outstanding designers of furniture, fabrics, and accessories. This photograph, of Filippo Perego's salon, offers an idea of the tributes I love to pay in the store to my international colleagues, presenting displays of their latest, most ground-breaking, and trendsetting creations.

It's also a great pleasure to introduce designers to America. Here are three photographs of Andrée Putman's first boutique, at Marshall Field's. It includes Andrée's own work, and pieces inspired by Eileen Gray, Gaudí, René Herbst, and Mariano Fortuny.

Marella Agnelli

I can't lavish enough respect or praise on my friend and colleague Marella Agnelli. I've had the stimulating pleasure of working with her on the design of several fabric collections. On the left, you see us reviewing some of her designs.

Here you see the fruits of my collaboration with Marella Agnelli: two settings in the store that capture the timeless elegance and warmth of a Romantic Italian interior.

A few samples of the designs that resulted from my joyous work with Marella Agnelli.

Art Interiors
1021 N. Main St.
Wheaton, IL 60187
Fine art

Baker Furniture
1661 Monroe
Grand Rapids, MI 49502
Furniture

Bamboo Odyssey
1225 S. Jellick
Rowland Heights, CA 91748
Wicker

Mike Bell
12-110 Merchandise Mart
Chicago, IL 60654

60 E. 10th St.
New York, NY 10003

8784 Beverly Blvd.
Los Angeles, CA 90048
*Antique furniture
and accessories*

Chapman Manufacturing Co. Inc.
481 W. Main St.
Avon, MA 02322
Lamps

Cocheo
306 E. 61st St.
New York, NY 10021
Furniture

Thayer Coggin
230 South Road
P. O. Box 5867
High Point, NC 27262
Furniture

Greg Copeland
10-14 Courtland Street
Paterson, NJ 07503
Fine art

Daly Design
117 Catamaran
Marina Del Rey, CA 90292
Fine art

Donghia
485 Broadway
New York, NY 10016
Furniture

Flair
P. O. Box 740
Lenoir, NC 28645
Furniture

Fur Design Interiors
Western Merchandise Mart, Space 436
San Francisco, CA 94103
*Antlers, animal skins,
mounted animal skins*

Hart Associates
P. O. Box 1387
McDonald Ave.
Ruston, LA 71270
Lamps

From the Jewel Collection for Thayer Coggin: the Diamond Chaise.

Henredon
P. O. Box 70
Morganton, NC 28655
Furniture

Hickory Chair
Hickory, NC 28603
Furniture

Interior Crafts
614 Merchandise Mart
Chicago, IL 60654
Furniture

Jason-Richards
363 W. Chicago Ave.
Chicago, IL 60610
Florist

P. Kaufmann, Inc.
51 Madison Avenue
New York, NY 10010
Fabrics

Kohler Co.
444 Highland Dr.
Kohler, WI 53044
Bathroom fixtures

Andrew Kolb & Son Ltd.
112 Madison Ave.
New York, NY 10016
Oil paintings

Karen Love and Associates
P. O. Box 96
Beverly Shore, IN 46301
Drapery

Marshall Field's
 Illinois Stores:
Chicago, Rockford, Aurora, Vernon Hills,
Lake Forest, Joliet, Oakbrook, Skokie,
Orland Park, Park Forest, Calumet City,
West Dundee, Bloomindale, Schaumburg

 Texas Stores:
Houston, Dallas, San Antonio

 Wisconsin Stores:
Milwaukee, Appleton, Madison, Wauwatosa
Total home furnishings

Minasian
1244 Chicago
Evanston, IL 60202
Antique Oriental carpets,
area carpets

News Metal Crafts, Inc.
812 N. Wells Street
Chicago, IL 60610
Antique and new
lighting fixtures

Niedermaier, Inc.
2828 N. Paulina
Chicago, IL 60657

435 Hudson St.
New York, NY 10014

8687 Melrose Ave., B 149
Los Angeles, CA 90069
Visual props, furniture,
and accessories

Pepper Construction
643 Orlen St.
Chicago, IL 60610
Contractor

Sirmos
47-07 30th Place
Long Island City, NY 11101
Furniture and accessories

Stark Carpet
979 3rd Ave.
New York, NY 10022
Carpets

Umbrello
8607 Melrose Avenue
Los Angeles, CA 90069
Furniture and accessories

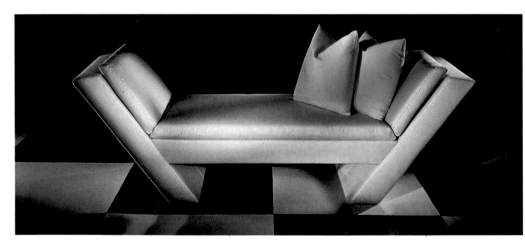

A sofa called Refractions, from the Jewel Collection.

ASIA

Enayoski Transom
Osaka, Japan
Transom

Fuso
6-47 Akasaka 7
Minato Ku, Tokyo, Japan
Lanterns

Heian Art
Sanjyo Hignshiyan-Ku
Kyoto 605, Japan
Roof tiles

Karumi Antiques
9-6-14 Akasaka Minato-Ku
Tokyo, Japan
Antiques

Kinnaree Co.
1163-1165 New Road
Bangkok 5, Thailand
Bronzes

Kyo Trading Co.
Sanjo-dari
East Jingumicki
Kyoto 605, Japan
Lanterns, pagodas

National Arts & Crafts Association
Beijing Branch
Beijing, China
Ceramic and porcelain

National Arts & Crafts Association
Shanghai Branch
Shanghai, China
Coromandel screens

Neold
145-12 Gaysorn Rd.
Rajaprasong
Bangkok, Thailand
Lacquerware and baskets

Okura Oriental Art
3-3-14 Azabudai
Tokyo, Japan
*Antique wood
shrines*

Sasakura
Osaka, Japan
Antique fireman's uniform

Tonoicki
Kyoto, Japan
Obi and kimonos

Yakoyama Inc.
Nawate, Higashiyama-Ku
Kyoto, Japan
*Scale models (houses),
obi, kimonos*

ENGLAND

La Barr
116 South St.
Leominster
Herefordshire
Antique pine furniture

M & L Silver
131 Whitechapel
London
Antique silver

Foreign Resources

Keith Skeel
94 Islington High Street
London
Antiques

Victoria Framing Services
Long Spring
Porterswood, St. Albans
Hertfordshire
Antique oils

*Forever in search of new design ideas: on a trip
to Beijing.*

Researching in Nuremburg with Susanna Selmin of Florence, and Robert Doerr of Chicago.

FRANCE

Herve Baume
19 Rue Petite Fusterie
84000 Avignon
Antiques

Facoglace
24 Passage Saint-Bernard
75011 Paris
Mirrors

Souleiado
78 Rue de Seine
75006 Paris
Fabrics

ITALY

Paggiali Agnelli
Via Sombre 40
50061 Compiobbi
Firenze
Steel furniture

Bartolozzi-Maioli
Via Maggio—13 Rosso
50125 Firenze
*Wood furniture
and accessories*

Bertini
Via Giuseppe Di Vittorio
N. 30
50055 Lastra Asigna
Firenze
Ceramics

Ceramiche d'Arte Bianchini
Loc. Cascine Del Riccio
50020 (Monte Oriolo)
Firenze
Ceramics

Filli Boffi S.N.C.
Viale Industria 5
20030 Tentate S/S
Milano
Furniture

F.P. II Italia
Via Bigli
20121 Milan
*Furniture and
accessories*

Gino Cenedese e Figlio
d. Duro 173
30121 Murano Venezia
Glass

Franco La Pina
Via Grosseto, 5-7
50142 Firenze
Silver

M.I.T.A.L.
Via Cappello, 31
Impruneta, Firenze
Terra cotta

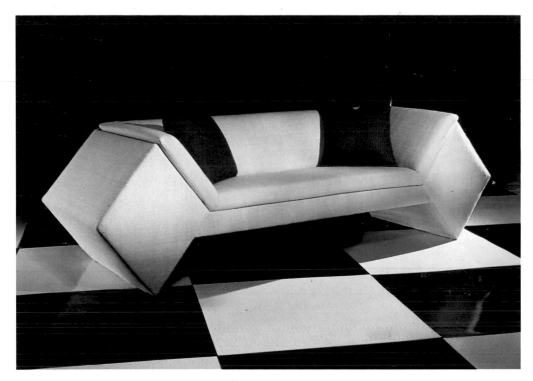

The Diamond Sofa from my Jewel Collection for Thayer Coggin.

Another view of Refractions from the Jewel Collection.

Morseletto
Via Dell'Economia, 97
36100 Vicenza
Vicenza stone sculptures

Pivato
Ceramiche Maiolichi
36055 Nove, Vicenza
*"Field Flowers";
ceramics*

San Marco
Via Segavecchia, 46
36055 Nove, Vicenza
Ceramics

Sellaro
Via Gozza
Pian di Marastica
Bassano
*Pine furniture, pine doors,
pine mantels*

Zichele
Via Vittoria 75
36065 Mussolente (VI)
Furniture

SPAIN

Moble-Antic
Los Centelles No. 17
46006 Valencia
Pine furniture

Roble Decoración
C/En Provecto, S/N
46721 Potries-Valencia
Furniture and accessories

Acknowledgments

Special thanks to Philip B. Miller for his total support, for allowing me to turn my fantasies into reality, and for the preface of *Epoustouflant*.

And my gratitude to my staff: Ron Fiore, Mara Forney, Thom Theis, Lydia Levanovic, Terri Labeau, Catherine Lapeyre, Agathe Marca, John Laycock, and the late Robert Doerr.

To Marella Agnelli, Franca Bini, Susanna Selmin, Mary Lou Tapinasi, Anne Beddow, Lord and Lady Wedgwood of Barlaston, Sir Humphrey Wakefield, Emilio Bergman, Nicole Fischelis, Jean Pierre Demery, Christiane Demery, Regine Demery, and Stephanie Demery, Keith Skeel, Andrée Putman, Filippo Perego, and all my friends across the Atlantic and the Pacific for their enthusiasm and support.

With acknowledgments to my friends and colleagues: Anne Gorman Miller, Eleanor Lambert Berkson, Christina Johnson Wolff, Sy Stewart, Helmut Horn and Cristina Tabora Horn, Jerry Seiff, Vito Ursini, Thayer Coggin, Herb Kohler, Natalie Black, Rod Kreitzer, Bill Peterson, Joseph Mrozek, Judy Niedermaier, Larry Kolb, Charlotte Simmons, John Mascheroni, Mark Hampton, Harry Root, George Philip Kelly and Marilyn Kelly, George Love and Lisa Love, Janet Connor, John Solimine and Pam Solimine, HO Finkelman and Reggie Finkelman, Angelo Arena and Alice Arena, Donald Norton, and the late Angelo Donghia.

And to my publisher, Len Forman, and to Claudia Forman, Beth Greenfeld, the very talented Norman Kolpas, Susan Shankin, Stan Last, and Linda O'Brien for their dedication and hard work.

To Deborah Daly of Daly Design, for her vision, unparalleled energy, and devotion to this project. Without her expertise, this book would not be a reality.

And special recognition to Hedrich-Blessing, to Jon Miller for his unerring eye, and to additional photographers: Nick Merrick, John Hedrich, Bill Hedrich, Bob Shimer, Jim Hedrich, Bob Harr, Scott McDonald, and Marco Lorenzetti. And to Jason Spohn, of Jason-Richards Florist, Chicago.

Endpapers and half-title fabric: "Geometric" from the Itamaki Collection

Title-page ceramic collection: "Field Flowers," designed by David Snyder, and manufactured by Pivato, Bassano, Italy.

Copyright page: Shibui lamps designed by David Snyder for Omero.

Part-title fabric: "Itamaki" from the Itamaki Collection, manufactured by P. Kaufmann, Inc. Designed by David Snyder.

Note: A few of the interiors in this book display skins of wild animals. I use only old skins, found by me in antique stores. I find the current illegal hunting of endangered species unconscionable, and I will not use any new skins in my collections.

Typography by JT&A Typographic Communication, Los Angeles.